THE UGLY BUG

By,
Tutu Mele

The Ugly Bug

By-

Tutu Mele

DEDICATION

This book is dedicated to all boys and girls who are learning about nature. They will love reading about this caterpillar as he changes into a butterfly. If your child is interested in nature, they will love following this caterpillar as he dreams of his journey and changes into a beautiful butterfly.

It is also dedicated to my grandchildren who are just starting school and learning to read. I hope it brings many years of reading pleasure to all preschool and beginning readers. Whether your child can read or likes to be read to, he or she will love this book.

Thank you to my good friend and author, Rhonda Feltman, for helping me get my children's books published. Thank you to all the children who are interested in nature and question how and why things go through changes.

By,
Tutu Mele

I am an ugly bug.
I am fat.
I am sick green.
I am sad.

I am so full.
I can eat so much.
I am so fat.
I want to look good.
That bug can fly so fast.
I am so slow.

I am tired now.
I want to go to sleep.
My bed is so soft and warm.
I like it when the wind blows.
It rocks me to sleep.
Sweet dreams!

What a great dream.
I would love to have that shirt.
Those pants are so full of color.
They are just my size.
I want to wear them now.

What great shades.
Hats! Hats! Hats!
I love hats!
They will cover my green head.
I will look so cool in these!

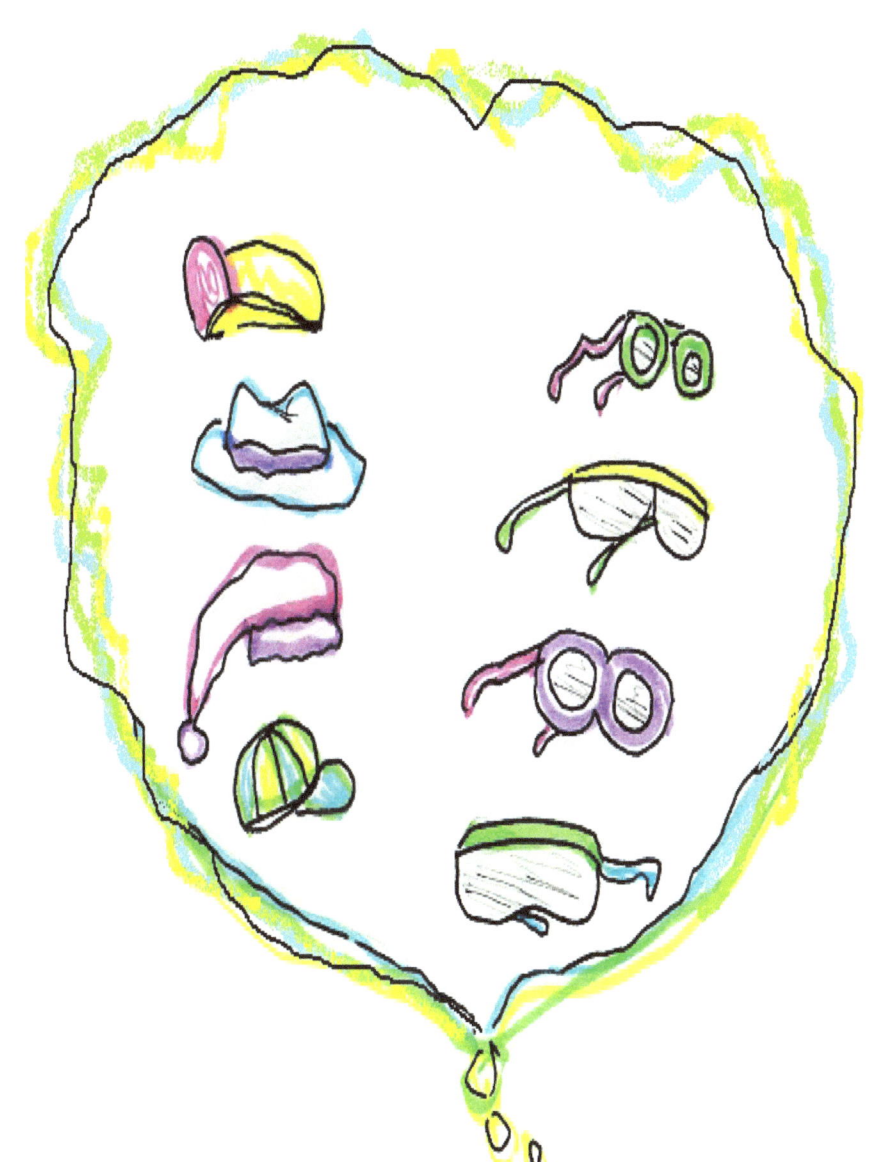

I want to have a hard body.
I want to move and groove.
I hope I get those new
clothes.
I hope this dream never
ends.

The sun feels so warm.
Time to wake up.
I need to move.
I feel great.
Naps are good for bugs.

Can this be true?
Can this be me?
Look at my pretty colors!
I am a new bug!
I am so colorful and pretty.
My dream came true.

I am so full of color.
No more green for me!
Now I can move and groove.
The sky is my home.
I am a glad bug!

Tutu Mele

This book is dedicated to my grandchildren who are learning to read and love the excitement of nature and the outdoors. They love hunting for caterpillars and butterflies and this book teaches them all about the life cycle of the butterflies that they catch.

This book is for all the budding naturalists in every family.

Whether your child can read or enjoys being read to, he or she will enjoy this book.

Tutu Mele loves writing books for the child that is beginning to read. She lives in Arizona for the summer and in Baja California in the winter. She is surrounded and inspired by nature to write these fun books.

The Ugly Bug
Vocabulary

the	ugly	bug	sweet
am	an	fat	sick
green	sad	so	full
want	look	good	he
fast	tired	now	bed
my	sleep	soft	rocks
wind	shirts	clothes	sale
pants	what	dream	have
that	those	color	great
shades	hats	love	cover
hard	body	move	be
never	ends	sun	feels
warm	move	need	naps
groove	new	this	sky
glad	home	wake	up

This book is part of a nature series.
Other titles by Tutu Mele include:

The Ugly Bug

The Frog That Croaked

Changing Colors

Little Whale Small

Little Kuapio Hohola

Little Whale Down Under

The Bike That Ate Dirt

Little Dog Laugh